Divine Mercy's
Prescription for
Spiritual Health

Divine Mercy's Prescription for Spiritual Health

Rev. George W. Kosicki, C.S.B.

Our Sunday Visitor Publishing Division
Our Sunday Visitor, Inc.
Huntington, Indiana 46750

Thanks

To Vinny Flynn for the inspiration and challenge
to write on the spirituality of St. Faustina.

To Father Ed Sylvia, C.S.C., and my brother Witold
for their helpful suggestions on the description
of the human condition.

To Christine Kruszyna for her patient perseverance
in preparing the manuscript.

To Sister Mary Ann Follmar for her
encouragement and support.

Not even the fangs of poisonous reptiles
overcame your sons, for your mercy
brought the antidote to heal them.
WISDOM 16:10

Jesus has a remedy for everything.
ST. FAUSTINA (Diary, 447)

CONTENTS

New Saint for a New Millennium

On Divine Mercy Sunday, April 30, 2000, Sister Maria Faustina of the Most Blessed Sacrament became the first saint of the Jubilee Year ushering in the third millennium. Known as the Apostle of Divine Mercy, she deeply understood the Merciful Heart of Jesus and knew that she was to be an instrument of His healing love. He had told her:

I do not want to punish aching mankind, but I desire to heal it. (Diary, 1588)

On the day of My feast, the Feast of Mercy, you will go through the world and bring fainting souls to the spring of My mercy. I shall heal and strengthen them. (Diary, 206)

FOREWORD

Divine Mercy's Prescription for Spiritual Health offers specific remedies for the unavoidable stress and suffering that fill our lives, and for the unhealthy tendencies and attitudes that so often plague us, spreading through our systems like poison.

Father Kosicki identifies twelve common human ailments — twelve "poisons" that can weaken or even destroy us in mind, body, heart, and soul.

For each of these ailments, he prescribes an antidote, drawn from the spirituality of St. Faustina. So, for the poison we call "fear," for example, the antidote from Faustina is "trust."

Each of the twelve antidotes is reinforced by Scripture passages and by excerpts from the diary of St. Faustina. Father Kosicki also adds his own insights, showing how the antidotes can be used not only as ways to counteract the negative content of our lives but also as stepping stones that lead us to sanctity.

Please, don't just read this book. Use it to discover where you need God's healing touch, from day to day, and take regular doses of the medicine you need.

— VINNY FLYNN

INTRODUCTION

Divine Mercy — An Important Message for Our Time

On April 30, 2000, the Sunday after Easter, Pope John Paul II canonized Sister Faustina Kowalska. Some 250,000 people filled St. Peter's Square to overflowing.

I was privileged to be present that day, having organized a Jubilee Year pilgrimage. With me were fourteen priests from the United States, all of whom had promoted Divine Mercy. In a special way, our pilgrimage honored my brother, Father Bohdan, who was celebrating the fiftieth anniversary of his priestly ordination. (Father Bohdan had used the image of the Divine Mercy on his ordination card years before the devotion was as popular as it is today.)

At the Mass of canonization, John Paul II not only canonized St. Faustina, but to our jubilant surprise he also "canonized" the whole Divine Mercy Message and Devotion by proclaiming the Sunday after Easter as Divine Mercy Sunday for the universal Church!

My fellow pilgrim-priests challenged me to write a catechesis about Mercy Sunday, to explain what the Holy Father did by the two-fold canonization. I did this in the form of a question-and-answer booklet titled *Why Mercy Sunday?* which was published by the Marian Press in Stockbridge, Massachusetts.

In that booklet, I explained the urgency of the message of Divine Mercy as proclaimed by John Paul II in his homily for the canonization of St. Faustina.

Three times during his homily he emphasized that St. Faustina's canonization and this message of Divine Mercy is "God's gift to our time." He went on to say that this gift of mercy will be particularly needed in the third millennium. He even said that Divine Mercy forms the "bridge from the second to the third millennium" and described it as the message "for our time."

On the first anniversary of St. Faustina's canonization, April 22, 2001, the Holy Father again celebrated Divine Mercy Sunday in St. Peter's Square and called that day the "Feast of Divine Mercy."

About This Book

The thought of using the Divine Mercy Message given to St. Faustina from Our Lord as a healing remedy originated some years ago. At the time, Vinny Flynn, former editor of the *Marian Helpers Bulletin*, asked me to write an article on the spiritual life of Sister Faustina, as found in her diary. Originally, that article looked at six characteristics of St. Faustina's life; over time, I expanded it to twelve. In a moment of inspiration, I realized that each of these twelve characteristics was an answer to a sickness of our secularized age.

Another moment of insight came to me while reading the Bible. In the Book of Wisdom, God's mercy is described as a healing remedy to the poisonous bite of the fiery serpents that Moses and the Israelites encountered in the desert:

Thy sons were not conquered even by the teeth of venomous serpents, for thy mercy came to their help and healed them. (Wis 16:10, Revised Standard Version)

Around the same time, I asked the student counselors at the Franciscan University of Steubenville what they found to be the most consistently mentioned problem of the students there. They agreed that by far, more than all other problems, the students had to deal with their fears: fear of the future, fear of failure, fear of success, fear of the past, and the list goes on.

What is the remedy to fear? TRUST! The remedy is found in Sacred Scripture and in the message of Divine Mercy. So "Fear vs. Trust" is at the top of the list of twelve poisons and their remedies.

Just reading the Table of Contents of this book and reviewing the list of the poisons and their remedies is like an examination of conscience. I've often read the list of poisons in the Table of Contents to people, and many of them freely admit, "I have them all!" You may find the same is true for you, or perhaps one or the other seems more relevant at the present moment.

This is a book to be read as the need arises. The twelve chapters can be read in any sequence. Each stands alone offering advice and help in dealing with whatever you may be struggling with at the present time. Read whatever prescription you need for your present spiritual health.

Divine Mercy's Prescription for Spiritual Health

This present book shows how the message of Divine Mercy is the healing prescription for our age and for the whole world!

The Divine Mercy Message and Devotion is strong and effective medicine for our age *and* is a response and fulfillment of the *mission* of St. Faustina to proclaim God's mercy.

Our Lord gave a mission to St. Faustina to:

- *Proclaim His mercy* to the whole world (see Diary, 1142).
- *Encourage souls* to trust in God's mercy (see Diary, 1690).
- *Tell aching mankind* to snuggle close to the Merciful Heart of Jesus (see Diary, 1074)
- *Tell the world that only by trust* in His mercy will mankind find peace (see Diary, 300).
- *Tell the greatest sinners* that they can reach great sanctity if only they would trust in His mercy (see Diary, 1784).
- *Prepare the world* for His second coming (see Diary, 429, 635).

Examine each of the twelve poisons of this secularized age and you will know that you, too, need the healing of Divine Mercy's prescription for spiritual health.

— REV. GEORGE W. KOSICKI, C.S.B.
August 15, 2001
Assumption of the Blessed Virgin Mary

HOW TO USE THIS BOOK

This is a "how-to" book. It shows how to respond to your day-by-day human condition and how to become an apostle of Divine Mercy like St. Faustina.

Each day may find you in a different situation or mood that calls for a different way of responding. This book can be a companion to help you discern, by the light of the Holy Spirit, the most fruitful response to the present moment.

The antidotes presented here can be taken as pills every time we need them, or like time-release capsules, to provide continuing protection. The antidotes build up our spiritual immune systems and shield us from the onslaught of human weakness and sin.

Each of the antidotes is a decision, an act of the will, to do something or not to do something. At times, it is a prayer, a short phrase we repeat over and over again from the heart. At other times, it is an invitation to the Lord, or permission we give to Him so that He can freely act. Or it may be a silent presence of heart to the Lord, who is present in our hearts . . . a decision to unite our hearts with His . . . a moment of loving union with the Lord, who loves us and is present to us by His Holy Spirit. It is always an act of mercy by deed, word, or prayer (see Diary, 742).

In various situations and times, we may well use more than one antidote at a time. It is not unusual to move from one to another as we respond to our varying human situations; and yet we all have experienced special moments of such darkness and weakness that we need all twelve antidotes at the same time! All the antidotes are available to us at any time and in any situation. They are gifts given to us to be used!

As we use these twelve antidotes to counteract our human misery, they become stepping stones that lead us across the mire of our human condition to spiritual growth, maturity, and interior peace. They transform us, step by step, into apostles of God's mercy — into living Eucharist — so that we may radiate His mercy by the witness of our lives.

These antidotes were gleaned from the diary of St. Faustina, *Divine Mercy in My Soul*, and they summarize her spiritual life.

But they are not unique to St. Faustina; rather, they are fundamental to a life lived in union with Christ, and many Christians have been transformed by them. St. Faustina is unique, however, in her special union with Christ as His secretary of Divine Mercy. Recording everything the Lord taught her, along with her own responses to these teachings, she describes not only the moments of ecstatic grace but also the dark and miserable moments.

Thanks be to God for this record of the human condition and her response to it, because all this helps us to identify with her in our struggle for spiritual growth. Her honest record of how she used the antidotes as strong medicine against negative attitudes and situations, and as stepping stones to sanctity, is an inspiration and a challenge to all of us who want to be transformed into apostles of Divine Mercy.

chapter ONE

FEAR

Being anxious, worried; afraid of death,
the future, the unknown, sickness,
violence, people.

vs.

Trust

Having a living faith in Jesus,
knowing that He is in charge,
and that He loves us.

Scriptural Response

"Fear is useless. What is needed is trust." (Mk 5:36)

"It is I. Do not be afraid!" (Mt 14:27)

Perfect love casts out all fear. (1 Jn 4:18)

Response from St. Faustina

The graces of My mercy are drawn by means of one vessel only, and that is trust. The more a soul trusts, the more it will receive. Souls that trust boundlessly are a great comfort to Me. . . . I pour all the treasures of My graces into them. (Words of Jesus, Diary, 1578)

Mankind will not have peace until it turns with trust to My mercy. (Words of Jesus, Diary, 300)

When my soul is in anguish, I think only in this way: Jesus is good and full of mercy, and even if the ground were to give way under my feet, I would not cease to trust in Him. (Diary, 1192)

Trust as a Stepping Stone to Sanctity

Trust is a living faith in the Lord, faith that He is indeed Lord, that He is in charge, and that He loves us with an infinite merciful love.

Trust gives God permission to act freely so He can have mercy on all (see Rom 11:32). Lack of trust is the greatest obstacle to God acting, and it is what pains Him the most. Souls do not trust Him and so do not receive His mercy.

Our Lord told St. Faustina that **the greatest sinners would achieve great sanctity, if only they would trust in My mercy** (Diary, 1784). "If only" is the key. If only souls would trust, they would overcome the obstacles of the human condition and take steps to grow spiritually.

The greatest obstacle of our human condition is fear. Fear paralyzes us and keeps us in bondage. The list of the fears and anxieties that plague us would fill a book! Yet Our Lord said in the gospel: "Fear is useless. What is needed is trust" (Mk 5:36).

How do we trust in the midst of fears? How do we use trust as an antidote to our fears and as a stepping stone to sanctity? What can you and I do?

We can repeat over and over again, from the heart, "Jesus, I trust in You!" That says it all. It is our way of living as Christians; it is our response to Jesus, who is mercy itself, who stands at the door of our hearts waiting for us to open them even a little bit (see Rv 3:20 and Diary, 1486, 1507).

"Jesus, I trust in You!" is the response Jesus asks of us in return for His blessing of merciful love. He asked that the image of Himself as the Merciful Savior be signed "Jesus, I trust in You!" This image of Jesus is a vessel with which we "gather" mercy; it is a reminder to trust in Him.

So how can you grow in TRUST? Gaze upon the image of the Merciful Savior often. Carry it with you, place it in your home and office, and even on the dashboard of your car — and cry out from your heart each time you look at it: "Jesus, I trust in You!"

Place all your fears into His Merciful Heart and trust. Open the doors of your heart and trust Jesus!

In the midst of the battle cry, shout the victory cheer: T.R.U.S.T.!

Total
Reliance
Upon
Saving
Truth

"If you continue in my word . . . you will know the truth, and the truth will make you free. . . . If the Son makes you free, you will be free indeed" (Jn 8:31-32, 36, Revised Standard Version).

JESUS, I TRUST IN YOU

Anyone can . . . look at this image of the merciful Jesus, His Heart radiating grace, and hear in the depths of his own soul what Blessed Faustina heard: "Fear nothing. I am with you always" (Diary, 586). And if this person responds with a sincere heart, "Jesus, I trust in You," he will find comfort in all his anxieties and fears.

— POPE JOHN PAUL II

chapter TWO

SHAME
Feeling inadequate, unworthy, unlovable, sinful, dirty, burdened by past sins and failures.

vs.

Mercy

Turning to God's mercy, accepting it, being transformed by it, and letting it flow out to others.

Scriptural Response

"We must celebrate and rejoice, because your brother was dead and has come to life again." (Lk 15:32)

"Be merciful, even as your Father is merciful." (Lk 6:36, Revised Standard Version)

"Blessed are the merciful, for they shall obtain mercy." (Mt 5:7, Revised Standard Version)

Response from St. Faustina

I am mercy itself. (Words of Jesus, Diary, 1739; see also 281, 300, 1074, 1148, 1273, 1777)

I understood that the greatest attribute is love and mercy. It unites the creature with the Creator. This immense love and abyss of mercy are made known in the Incarnation of the Word and in the Redemption [of humanity], and it is here that I saw this as the greatest of all God's attributes. (Diary, 180)

I am giving you three ways of exercising mercy toward your neighbor: the first — by deed, the second — by word, the third — by prayer. (Words of Jesus, Diary, 742)

My mercy is greater than your sins and those of the entire world. (Words of Jesus, Diary, 1485)

Mercy as a Stepping Stone to Sanctity

Mercy is God's love poured out upon us miserable sinners, love poured through His pierced Heart as a fount of mercy for us. It is love's second name (see Pope John Paul II, *Rich in Mercy*, 7).

A victory cheer capsulizes mercy as God Himself:

Mighty
Eternal
Redeeming
Compassionate
Yahweh

Our Lord taught St. Faustina that He is mercy itself, that His mercy is like a vast, bottomless ocean. It is greater than all our sins, all our fears, all our anxieties, all our darkness and depression; and it is available to everyone:

Urge all souls to trust in the unfathomable abyss of My mercy, because I want to save them all. On the cross, the fountain of My mercy was opened wide by the lance for all souls — no one have I excluded! (Diary, 1182)

Write that I am more generous toward sinners than toward the just. (Diary, 1275)

God's mercy is always available. His plan and His desire is to have mercy on all (see Rom 11:32). He wants no one to escape His mercy. But, because of our free will, we can frustrate His plan by not accepting His mercy.

One of the greatest obstacles to accepting His mercy is our shame. Because of our past sins and failures, we feel unlovable, unworthy, dirty, miserable, distressed, distrustful, anxious, and tormented. Shame is the response of Adam and Eve to their sin. Shame is the most common response of those who have sinned and turned away from God's mercy.

And yet there is something worse than our shame and sin: not turning to the mercy of God after we have sinned. The Lord waits for us to turn to Him, just as the father waits for his prodigal son (see Lk 15:11-32). By His mercy, the Lord wants to restore our dignity, our worth, and our value. This is cause for rejoicing (see Pope John Paul II, *Rich in Mercy*, 5-6).

The antidote to shame is mercy — God's Divine Mercy. This antidote becomes a stepping stone to transformation and sanctity as we turn to His mercy, accept it, let it transform us, and let it flow out to others.

The Lord commands us to use His mercy, to be merciful even as our heavenly Father is merciful (see Lk 6:36). We are to be merciful to others by deed, word, and prayer (see Diary, 742). As we are merciful to others, we ourselves obtain more mercy: "Blessed are the merciful, for they shall obtain mercy" (Mt 5:7, Revised Standard Version); and at the same time, we are merciful to the Lord Himself (see Mt 25:40; Pope John Paul II, *Rich in Mercy*, 8).

How can I be merciful in a practical way? By humbly doing the Corporal and Spiritual Works of Mercy.

The Corporal Works of Mercy are feeding the hungry, giving drink to the thirsty, clothing the naked, sheltering the travelers, comforting the prisoners, visiting the sick, and burying the dead.

The Spiritual Works of Mercy include teaching the ignorant, praying for the living and the dead, correcting the sinners, counseling those in doubt, consoling the sorrowful, bearing wrongs patiently, and forgiving wrongs willingly.

The following prayer for mercy is always a practical and effective way to receive and use God's mercy as a stepping stone toward transformation and sanctity:

> Jesus, fill me with Your mercy, that I may be merciful,
> that I may radiate Your mercy. Jesus, Mercy!

The prayer "Jesus, Mercy!" is not only a plea for mercy on us and on the whole world; it is also a cry of praise and thanksgiving for Jesus, who is mercy itself. This prayer should arise from our hearts as a continuous plea for mercy, especially as we see the shame, sin, and misery in our own lives and in the lives of all in the world.

chapter THREE

REBELLION

Being angry, full of hatred,
unwilling, judgmental,
unforgiving, aggressive.

vs.

God's Will

Seeking to live in joyful acceptance
of God's will, desiring His will
above all else.

Scriptural Response

"Your will be done." (Mt 6:10; 26:42)

"I have come to do your will." (Heb 10:9)

"Not everyone who says to me, 'Lord, Lord,' will enter the kingdom of heaven, but only the one who does the will of my Father in heaven." (Mt 7:21)

Response from St. Faustina

The Lord Jesus gave me to know how very pleasing to Him is a soul who lives in accordance with the will of God. It thereby gives very great glory to God. (Diary, 821; see also 724, 952)

There is one word I heed and continually ponder; it alone is everything to me; I live by it and die by it, and it is the holy will of God. It is my daily food. My whole soul listens intently to God's wishes. I do always what God asks of me, although my nature often quakes and I feel the magnitude of these things is beyond my strength. I know well what I am of myself, but I also know what the grace of God is, which supports me. (Diary, 652)

God's Will as a Stepping Stone to Sanctity

"Your will be done" (Mt 6:10) is the prayer that Jesus taught us and the prayer that He lived: "Take this cup away from me, but not what I will but what you will" (Mk 14:36). Jesus came to do the will of His Father (see Heb 10:9): "My food is to do the will of the one who sent me and to finish his work" (Jn 4:34).

Mary, our Blessed Mother, expressed this submission to the will of God at the Annunciation: "May it be done to me according to your word" (Lk 1:38). St. Paul expressed his submission by saying, "It is no longer I who live, but Christ who lives in me" (Gal 2:20, Revised Standard Version).

St. Faustina was instructed by Our Lord to cross out her own will in a graphic way:

> **Write these words on a clean sheet of paper: "From today on, my own will does not exist," and then cross out the page. And on the other side write these words: "From today on, I do the Will of God everywhere, always, and in everything."** (Diary, 372)

The contact point of God's will and our will is the point of interaction of God's freedom and our freedom. God's glory is that He created us free, and that He will not violate that freedom. He asks, invites, encourages, cajoles, knocks, and waits for us to act freely in submitting to His will, where we find real freedom. This is the very paradox of the gospel

— in dying, we are born to eternal life. When we die to our self-will, we find eternal life in His will.

What is the result when we focus on our own will? Rebellion! A rebellious attitude that echoes the cry of Lucifer: "I will not serve!" A rebellion that expresses itself in anger, hatred, cursing, self-righteous judgments and questioning, self-reliance, and self-determination. This rebellion is the root of all sin.

And what is the antidote to our rebellious spirit? God's will. As we seek God's will and actually do it, we take steps to transformation and sanctity. The basic issue is: "Your will be done." There are two parts to it: first, that it be God's will and not just mine or others'; and secondly, that it actually be done according to His plan and timing.

But then comes the important question: What is God's will? What does God want for me, moment by moment, in my daily living?

- He wants us all to be saved and come to the knowledge of the truth (see 1 Tm 2:4).
- He wants to have mercy on all (see Rom 11:32).
- He wants to establish His Kingdom in our hearts by the Holy Spirit (see Mt 6:10; Rom 5:5).
- He wants us to obey His commandments (see Mt 19:16-26).
- He wants us to be merciful, even as He is merciful (see Lk 6:36).
- He wants us to love one another as He loves us (see Jn 13:34).

- He wants us to eat His flesh and drink His blood and have eternal life (see Jn 6:54).
- He wants us to obey His Church (see Mt 16:19; Jn 20:23).
- He wants us to live as members of His family (see Col 3:12-21).
- He wants us to call Him "Our Father," "Abba" (see Mt 6:9; Jn 20:17).
- He wants to give us His Holy Spirit (see Lk 10:13; 24:49; Acts 1:8).
- He wants us to take Mary as our mother (see Jn 19:26-27).
- He wants us to learn to be gentle and humble of heart (see Mt 11:28-29).

God's will is expressed throughout Sacred Scripture. One especially beautiful expression of it is found in the writings of St. Paul, who gives us a practical way of doing God's will moment by moment, using this antidote as a stepping stone to growth:

Rejoice always.
Pray without ceasing.
In all things give thanks, for this is the will
of God in Christ Jesus regarding you all.
(1 Thes 5:16-18, Confraternity Edition)

"This is the will of God . . . regarding you all." It is in the plural; it is the will of God for everybody, and at all

From today on,
my own will
does not exist.

From today on,
I do the Will of God
everywhere, always,
and in everything.

times, and it is always available for us. In this way, we can surrender our wills to His will, His plans, and His pleasure.

But what if I don't know God's will in a particular situation? I can still surrender my will to His by asking for light to see His will, and by praying for the strength to follow that will. When we use our free will to surrender to the will of God, He will certainly bless our decision by revealing that will to us.

Our battle cry in life, our antidote to our rebellious spirit, and our stepping stone to sanctity is: "Father, Your will be done!"

chapter FOUR

SELFISHNESS

Being self-centered, self-concerned, self-seeking, self-fulfilling, pleasure seeking.

vs.

Glorifying God's Mercy

Focusing on God instead of on ourselves, praising and proclaiming His mercy.

Scriptural Response

"Go home to your family and make it clear to them how much the Lord in his mercy has done for you." (Mk 5:19-20)

I will give thanks to you among the peoples, O LORD; I will chant your praise among the nations, for your kindness towers to the heavens, and your faithfulness to the skies. (Ps 108:4-5)

Response from St. Faustina

Give praise and glory to this mercy of Mine. (Words of Jesus, Diary, 206)

By this means [mercy toward others by deed, word, and prayer] a soul glorifies and pays reverence to My mercy. (Words of Jesus, Diary, 742)

I expect from you, My child, a great number of souls who will glorify My mercy for all eternity. (Words of Jesus, Diary, 1489)

I demand . . . that people revere My mercy. (Words of Jesus, Diary, 742)

Glorifying God's Mercy as a Stepping Stone to Sanctity

To glorify God's mercy is to reverence it and acknowledge it as His greatest attribute (see Pope John Paul II, *Rich in Mercy*, 14; Diary, 180). Glorifying the mercy of God was the very reason and purpose of St. Faustina's life: "Glorifying Your mercy," she wrote, "is the exclusive task of my life" (Diary, 1242). She glorified God's mercy in all her words, deeds, and prayers.

Glorifying God's mercy can be defined by a series of words that begin with the letter "p": *praising* it; *praying* for it; *pleading* for it; *proclaiming* it; and, especially, *practicing* mercy to others.

After His healing of the demoniac, Jesus shows that He wants His mercy glorified, telling the man to return to his home and tell his family about God's mercy to him (see Mk 5:19-20). To glorify God's mercy is to tell others what God has done for you, to tell your family, your friends, and anyone who will listen to you.

We all should tell others about God's desire to pour out His mercy, especially on sinners and on the miserable (see Diary, 723, 1275). We should tell them that His mercy is greater than all our sin and misery (see Diary, 699).

Like St. Faustina, who was conscious of her mission in the Church to constantly plead for mercy (see Diary, 482), we, too, can plead for mercy on the whole Church and world, and so glorify His mercy.

Like St. Faustina, we can write about His mercy or distribute leaflets about Divine Mercy.

We can also support with prayer and with funds those who are glorifying God's mercy by their writing and preaching. Pray especially for their strength and protection because they are in the front line of this spiritual warfare. Like St. Faustina, they know how Satan hates God's mercy (see Diary, 412, 520, 1496-1499).

Our Lord gave St. Faustina great promises for those who glorify His mercy:

All those souls who will glorify My mercy and spread its worship, encouraging others to trust in My mercy, will not experience terror at the hour of death. (Diary, 1540)

With those that glorify and proclaim My great mercy to others, I will deal according to My infinite mercy at the hour of their death. (Diary, 379)

In this book [of life] are written the names of the souls that have glorified My mercy. (Diary, 689)

Glorifying God's mercy is the antidote to our human condition of selfishness. Turning to God's mercy overcomes our self-seeking, self-concern, self-fulfillment, and pleasure seeking.

When we glorify God's mercy, we focus our lives on Him, instead of on ourselves, as number one. We then realize that God is God and we are not. When we turn to Him in our human condition, He can transform us into holy vessels of His great mercy.

Glorifying God's mercy is the precious golden door by which we enter into union with Him. It is the great response of the Blessed Mother in her Magnificat:

> "My soul proclaims the greatness of the Lord; my spirit rejoices in God my savior. . . . The Mighty One has done great things for me, and holy is his name. His mercy is from age to age." (Lk 1:46-47, 49-50)

chapter FIVE

SECULARIZATION
Living as though there were
no God, or being indifferent to
God (practical atheism).

vs.

Glorifying the Trinity

Living as children of God,
rejoicing in the Three Divine Persons
living in our hearts.

Scriptural Response

The proof that you are sons is the fact that God has sent forth
into our hearts the spirit of His Son which cries out "Abba!"
("Father!"). (Gal 4:6)

"Whoever loves me will keep my word, and my Father
will love him, and we will come to him and make our dwelling
with him. . . . The Advocate, the holy Spirit that the Father
will send in my name — he will teach you everything and
remind you of all that [I] told you." (Jn 14:23, 26)

Response from St. Faustina

I was drawn into the bosom of the Most Holy Trinity.
(Diary, 1670)

Jesus, when You come to me in Holy Communion,
You who together with the Father and the Holy Spirit
have deigned to dwell in the little heaven of my heart,
I try to keep You company throughout the day. (Diary,
486)

Glorifying the Trinity as a Stepping Stone to Sanctity

The most obvious impression upon reading the diary of St. Faustina, even a part of it, is that she lived in an intimate communion with God. She saw Him, talked to Him, listened to Him, suffered with Him, and loved Him with her whole heart, mind, and strength. God was all to her.

The message of her life is clear: God exists, He is real, He is present, He loves us, and He wants us to be united with Him.

In our human condition, we so easily live as though God doesn't exist. It is a form of practical atheism. At least the real atheist has the politeness to deny God. But in our age, so many live in indifference to Him. They glorify themselves in a parody of the Gloria: "Glory to man in the highest, and peace to the man with the most!"

The antidote to this secularization, to this forgetfulness of God, is to glorify Him — Father, Son, and Holy Spirit. We glorify God when we respond to the fact that He exists, that He is love, and that He wants to transform us in a loving union with Him. We respond to Him by praise, worship, thanksgiving, and love — a love of Him with our whole heart, mind, and strength, and a love of one another.

We glorify the Holy Trinity when we accept the love of the Father and the Son, poured into our hearts by the Holy Spirit (see Rom 5:5). The Father creating us, the Son redeeming us, and the Holy Spirit sanctifying us — all are gifts of mercy.

As we receive these gifts of mercy, we learn to live in an intimate relationship with each Person of the Trinity.

St. Faustina writes:

> Once after Holy Communion, I heard these words: **You are Our dwelling place.** At that moment, I felt in my soul the presence of the Holy Trinity: the Father, the Son, and the Holy Spirit. (Diary, 451)

And again, during a time of Eucharistic Adoration:

> I knew more distinctly than ever before the Three Divine Persons, the Father, the Son, and the Holy Spirit. My soul is in communion with these Three. . . .Whoever is united to One of the Three Persons is thereby united to the whole Blessed Trinity, for this Oneness is indivisible. (Diary, 472)

What should our response be for this wonderful gift? St. Faustina explains that we should glorify the Trinity by loving as God loves:

> The Holy Trinity grants me Its life abundantly, by the gift of the Holy Spirit. The Three Divine Persons live in me. When God loves, He loves with all His Being, with all the power of His Being. If God has loved me in this way, how should I respond — I, His spouse? (Diary, 392)

St. Faustina, from her experience of being drawn up into the bosom of the Most Holy Trinity and being immersed in the pure love of God (see Diary, 1121, 1129, 1670), teaches us how to use this antidote of glorifying the Holy Trinity as a stepping stone to sanctity:

> Today, I live, glorifying the Holy Trinity. I thank God that He has deigned to adopt us as His children, through grace. (Diary, 1819)

> O my Jesus, how very easy it is to become holy; all that is needed is a bit of good will. . . . Faithfulness to the inspirations of the Holy Spirit — that is the shortest route. (Diary, 291)

chapter SIX

MISERY

Being sick, in pain, inept,
unable, worried, anxious,
gloomy, dissipated, sinful.

vs.

Suffering for Others

Offering our here-and-now
sufferings and pain for others
in union with Jesus.

Scriptural Response

I rejoice in my sufferings for your sake, and in my flesh I complete what is lacking in Christ's afflictions for the sake of his body; that is, the church. (Col 1:24, Revised Standard Version)

Response from St. Faustina

I desire that you make an offering of yourself for sinners and especially for those souls who have lost hope in God's mercy. (Words of Jesus, Diary, 308)

Mother of God, your soul was plunged into a sea of bitterness; look upon your child and teach her to suffer and to love while suffering. (Diary, 315)

I am giving you a share in the redemption of mankind. (Words of Jesus, Diary, 310)

Oh, if only the suffering soul knew how it is loved by God, it would die of joy and excess of happiness! Some day, we will know the value of suffering, but then we will no longer be able to suffer. The present moment is ours. (Diary, 963)

Suffering for Souls as a Stepping Stone to Sanctity

The most obvious condition of mankind, the one that is common to all of us, is misery or suffering. We all have pain. None of us can escape it; it seems to be always with us. So what can we do about it? Our present society tells us to escape from it. Suffering and pain are to be eliminated as quickly as possible: seek out a pill, a doctor, a vacation, a pleasure that will distract you from the pain. The message is that pain is useless and without meaning.

The presence of suffering in the world is probably the greatest excuse for denying God. How can there be a merciful God who allows suffering? How can there be a God who wants innocent children to suffer? And the list of complaints goes on.

But there is another side to suffering. Suffering was the way God the Father chose for His Son, Jesus, to show us ultimate love and mercy, and ultimate humility. By His love, Jesus transformed suffering to bring salvation to all mankind. By His suffering, He Himself was "perfected . . . designated as high priest . . ." (see Heb 5:9-10; Pope John Paul II, *The Christian Meaning of Human Suffering*, February 11, 1984).

Then, Jesus extended His invitation to us to share in the work of redemption, to be partners with Him by offering our sufferings with love, united with Him as members of His Body: "All this is as God intends, for it is your special privilege to take Christ's part — not only to believe in him but also to suffer for him" (Phil 1:29).

How beautifully Pope John Paul II invited the more than five hundred sick on stretchers in St. Peter's Basilica to offer their sufferings for the Church leaders (February 11, 1984). The Holy Father went on to point out that Jesus taught us two things about suffering: one, to do good to those who suffer; and two, to do good with the suffering.

St. Paul could find his joy in the suffering he endured for our sake as he filled up in his own flesh what was lacking in the sufferings of Christ (see Col 1:24). How could Paul find joy in his suffering? Because he found meaning in suffering. It brings mercy and salvation to others (see Pope John Paul II, *The Christian Meaning of Human Suffering*, February 11, 1984).

What was lacking in the sufferings of Christ? He had not yet suffered in Paul, in you, and in me — He wanted to show the fullness of love and give us an opportunity to show love and share in the work of redemption. What a mystery! Christ lives and suffers in you and me: "the mystery of Christ in you, your hope of glory" (Col 1:27).

The key to suffering is suffering for others, for souls. When we offer our present, here-and-now sufferings and pain for others with love, united with Jesus, especially in the Eucharist, we do a meaningful, precious, and effective work of intercession and redemption. We bring God's mercy and salvation to souls in need. By our suffering for souls, we bring to them the mercy and salvation won for us on the cross by Jesus. We are ambassadors of Christ, bringing His reconciliation (see 2 Cor 5:20).

Suffering for souls is not masochism. We do not seek suffering for the sake of suffering itself but rather for the sake of others. We do not need to take on extra sufferings. There are plenty for all of us in our daily life! As a special grace, the Lord calls certain privileged souls to a more intensive suffering for souls, as He called St. Faustina. This grace must be responded to only under the direction of a spiritual director, and in humility.

Suffering for souls does not mean we neglect our health. We are to be good stewards of the bodies the Lord has given us and to take normal care for our physical, emotional, and spiritual health. Care for our health makes it possible for us to work effectively for the Kingdom of God and the salvation of souls.

How do we offer up our sufferings? What do we actually do? We make an act of the will and say with our heart:

> Lord Jesus, I offer You this pain, this misery, this suffering for souls. I offer it in union with Your passion, death, and resurrection offered at each Holy Mass.

Various ways can be used to express the offering. The point is to lovingly unite our suffering with the suffering of Christ — for souls. We can direct our offering to specific souls if we wish, naming the person(s) of our concern. The words are not essential; what is essential is the intention to offer our sufferings with Jesus for others.

> Jesus, for souls.
> Jesus, with You in Your passion.

Jesus, accept my pain for souls.

Jesus, I offer this _____ in love.

The offering of our suffering and pain will not take away the pain, but it will give it meaning and value. "How do we suffer?" asks Pope John Paul II. Then he answers his own question, "With great pain!" (*The Christian Meaning of Suffering*, February 11, 1984).

St. Peter writes: "There is cause for rejoicing here. You may for a time have to suffer the distress of many trials: but this is so that your faith, which is more precious than the passing splendor of fire-tried gold, may by its genuineness lead to praise, glory, and honor when Jesus Christ appears" (1 Pt 1:6-7).

St. Faustina learned the lesson of suffering for others from Our Lord. He asked her to make an offering of herself, uniting herself with His passion for the salvation of souls, especially sinners (see Diary, 135, 136, 137, 138, 186, 187, 190, 205, 206, 308, 309, 726). He wanted St. Faustina to be transformed by love:

I desire that you be entirely transformed into love and that you burn ardently as a pure victim of love.
(Diary, 726)

So, with complete obedience and faith, St. Faustina embraced suffering and came to know its value:

Suffering is a great grace; through suffering the soul becomes like the Savior; in suffering, love becomes crystallized; the greater the suffering, the purer the love. (Diary, 57)

Our Lord revealed to her the great mystery of suffering, telling her, "**I have need of your sufferings to rescue souls**" (Diary, 1612).

God needs our sufferings? Yes, God needs to continue His merciful outpouring of love through you and me. It seems that the love that Christ poured out on the world was not enough to show the depth and riches of His mercy; He wants to show that merciful love for souls through you and me! "It is your special privilege . . . to suffer for [Christ]" (Phil 1:29).

We can find our joy in that suffering for souls, just as St. Paul (see Col 1:24) and St. Faustina did. "From the moment I came to love suffering," Faustina explains, "it ceased to be a suffering for me. Suffering is the daily food of my soul" (Diary, 276). She even says that suffering can be "a delight," but only when love lends value to it (see Diary, 303, 351). Only love makes suffering valuable, precious, and a joy. What a mystery of love the Lord invites us to share!

Suffering for souls is the antidote to the human condition of misery. Suffering with love for souls, suffering with Christ, and allowing Christ to suffer in you is the stepping stone to transformation and sanctity.

Suffering is precious! Don't waste it. Offer it! — with love, with and in Christ, for souls. This is our privilege: to take Christ's part, to bring His mercy to souls.

chapter SEVEN

PRIDE

Being self-righteous,
self-centered, rebellious,
judgmental, resentful, boastful.

vs.

Humility

Realizing that God is God
and I am not. Being willing to
serve in humble, hidden ways.

Scriptural Response

"Learn from me, for I am gentle and humble of heart." (Mt 11:29)

"He has cast down the mighty from their thrones, and has lifted up the lowly." (Lk 1:52, International Consultation on English Texts)

Response from St. Faustina

Now I understand why there are so few saints; it is because so few souls are deeply humble. (Diary, 1306)

Humiliation is my daily food. (Diary, 92)

Nothing is better for the soul than humiliations. . . . If there is a truly happy soul upon earth, it can only be a truly humble soul. . . . A humble soul does not trust itself, but places all its confidence in God. (Diary, 593)

Humility as a Stepping Stone to Sanctity

Humility is not a popular virtue in our day. In fact, it's probably the most despised and ridiculed of virtues because it cuts to the heart of our human condition — pride. As sinful human beings, we are proud — self-righteous, self-centered, rebellious, resentful, and judgmental. Humility is the countersign to our proud age.

Because humility is the antidote to pride, it is the fundamental virtue of the spiritual life. Without humility, there is no spiritual life. Jesus took the way of humility to reveal the Father's mercy and bring us salvation. As St. Paul expresses it, "He humbled himself, obediently accepting even death, death on a cross! Because of this, God highly exalted him" (Phil 2:8-9).

St. Augustine, one of the great Doctors of the Church, considered humility the way to sanctity:

> I would wish that you place yourself with all your love under Christ, and that you pave no other way in order to reach and to attain the truth than has already been paved by Him who, as God, knows the weakness of our steps. This way is, in the first place, humility; in the second place, humility; in the third place, humility. . . . As often as you ask me about the Christian religion's norms of conduct, I choose to give no other answer than: humility. (Letter 118, 2, 11)

In our own century, our Blessed Mother echoed St. Augustine as she taught St. Faustina about virtue:

I desire, my dearly beloved daughter, that you practice the three virtues that are dearest to me — and most pleasing to God. The first is humility, humility, and once again humility. (Diary, 1415)

What is humility? First of all, it is the realization that God is God and I am not!

One key to humility is **"total gift"** — a gift of self and a gift of service. "God so loved the world that he gave his only Son" (Jn 3:16). God totally gave His Son as a sacrificial gift of love on the cross for us. Jesus expressed His humility in that He came "not to be served by others, but to serve, to give his own life as a ransom for the many" (Mt 20:28).

Another key to humility is **"other."** God is "other," and we love and serve Him; our neighbor is "other," and we love and serve him (or her). Humble, hidden, silent service is one of the great ways of expressing our humility — doing the simple tasks appropriate to our state of life; not blowing a trumpet to announce our great contribution, but doing the little things that no one else will see.

A third key to humility is **"transparency."** We are transparent when others see in us the Lord at work, when they see His mercy radiate from us, so that they are moved to give thanks to God. Transparency is characteristic of Jesus (when we look at Jesus, we see the Father — see Jn 14:9) and of Mary (she leads us to Jesus: "Do whatever he tells you" — Jn 2:5). With Mary, we can live the Magnificat, giving constant praise and thanks to God for the great things He has done for the humble (see Lk 1:46-55).

Only the humble can receive God's mercy. Only the emptied can be filled. Only in dying are we born to eternal life. Humility is the necessary condition for spiritual growth. How beautifully Jesus, who is truth itself, calls us to learn humility from Him:

> "Learn from me, for I am meek and humble of heart; and you will find rest for yourselves." (Mt 11:29)

Humility is the most needed antidote for sinful humanity, and it is the cornerstone of sanctity.

chapter EIGHT

SPIRITUAL WEAKNESS

Feeling fatigued, depressed, burdened, bored, lustful, intemperate, avaricious.

vs.

Eucharist

Taking time for "Radiation Therapy" before the Eucharist, allowing God to strengthen and transform us.

Scriptural Response

"He who feeds on my flesh and drinks
my blood has life eternal." (Jn 6:54)

Response from St. Faustina

O Blessed Host, in whom is contained the medicine
for all our infirmities. (Diary, 356)

The most solemn moment of my life is the moment
when I receive Holy Communion . . . and for every
Holy Communion I give thanks to the Most Holy
Trinity. (Diary, 1804)

Here is the tabernacle of Your mercy. Here is the
remedy for all our ills. (Diary, 1747)

All the good that is in me is due to Holy Communion.
I owe everything to it. I feel that this holy fire has
transformed me completely. (Diary, 1392)

Eucharist as a Stepping Stone to Sanctity

Taking bread and giving thanks, he broke it and gave it to them, saying: "This is my body to be given for you. Do this as a remembrance of me." He did the same with the cup after eating, saying as he did so: "This cup is the new covenant in my blood, which will be shed for you." (Lk 22:19-20)

The Eucharist is truly a miracle of mercy and of humility! God empties Himself in a total gift of merciful love so that we may be filled with His life: "Just as the Father who has life sent me and I have life because of the Father, so the man who feeds on me will have life because of me" (Jn 6:57).

Because of the Eucharist, we are transformed. We become what we eat — the living Body of the Lord. The Eucharist is the agent of transformation, from a merely human life to a mature life as members of the mystical Body of Christ. Eucharist brings to fullness the seed of life given to us in Baptism (see Decree on the Ministry and Life of Priests, 5).

St. Faustina, whose full religious name is Sister Maria Faustina of the Most Blessed Sacrament, prayed for this transformation:

Jesus, transform me, miserable and sinful as I am, into Your own self (for You can do all things), and give me to Your Eternal Father. I want to become a sacrificial host before You, but an ordinary wafer to people. (Diary, 483)

St. Faustina was so transformed by the Holy Eucharist, and by her total and humble giving of herself, that Our Lord said to her: **"You are a living host, pleasing to the Heavenly Father"** (Diary, 1826).

The Eucharist is the antidote to the human condition, the agent of transforming our human weakness into a living sacrifice offered for the salvation of souls. By it, we are transformed into living Eucharist, radiating His mercy.

We can learn from St. Faustina how to draw all our strength from the Eucharist:

One thing alone sustains me, and that is Holy Communion. From it I draw my strength; in it is all my comfort. . . . Jesus concealed in the Host is everything to me. From the tabernacle I draw strength, power, courage, and light. . . . I would not know how to give glory to God if I did not have the Eucharist in my heart. (Diary, 1037)

What can you and I do to use the Eucharist as an antidote to our untransformed human condition and as a stepping stone to mature sanctity? We can make His offering of Mass the center of our lives:

Taking part in the eucharistic sacrifice, which is the fount and apex of the whole Christian life, they [Christians] offer the Divine Victim to God, and offer themselves along with It. (Dogmatic Constitution on the Church, 11)

By Holy Orders, the priest consecrates the Eucharist; by Holy Baptism, we all offer the Divine Victim and receive Him in Holy Communion. By offering and receiving the Immaculate Victim, we are transformed.

We can continue our participation in this "miracle of mercy" (Diary, 1489) and come to this "fountain of mercy" (Diary, 1817) in the following ways: by a spiritual offering of our sufferings and pains in union with the Eucharistic sacrifice; by our spiritual communions that we make with our hearts, welcoming and thanking Jesus; and by our adoration of the Blessed Sacrament present on the altar and in the tabernacle. We can take extended times of adoration as a regular part of our spiritual life. We need these times of silent presence to the One who is radiantly present. We need to open our hearts to "Radiation Therapy," which transforms our human condition!

As the bread and wine are transubstantiated into the Body and Blood of the Lord, so we, too, are to be transformed. After the consecration, the priest invokes the Holy Spirit, that we may become the living Body of Christ:

Grant that we, who are nourished by his body and blood, may be filled with his Holy Spirit, and become one body, one spirit in Christ. (Eucharistic Prayer III)

As we are transformed by the Eucharist into the living Body of Christ, we become more and more a countersign to our age: we begin to radiate His holiness as a countersign to the loss of the sense of sin; and we radiate His humility and His mercy as a countersign to a proud and self-centered generation.

chapter NINE

GUILT

Being sinful, divided, unforgiving;
feeling unworthy, no-good,
bitter, despondent.

vs.

Reconciliation

Being reconciled to God
by confession and to one
another by mutual forgiveness.

Scriptural Response

"Nor do I condemn you. You may go. But from now on, avoid this sin." (Jn 8:11)

Be reconciled to God! (2 Cor 5:21)

Be kind to one another, compassionate, and mutually forgiving, just as God has forgiven you in Christ. (Eph 4:32)

Response from St. Faustina

When you approach the confessional, know this, that I myself am waiting there for you. I am only hidden by the priest, but I myself act in your soul. Here the misery of the soul meets the God of mercy. (Words of Jesus, Diary, 1602)

We come to confession to be healed; we come to be educated — like a small child, our soul has constant need of education. (Diary, 377)

Tell souls that from this fount of mercy souls draw graces solely with the vessel of trust. If their trust is great, there is no limit to My generosity. (Words of Jesus, Diary, 1602)

Reconciliation as a Stepping Stone
to Sanctity

St. Paul strongly implores us in the name of Christ, "Be reconciled to God!" (2 Cor 5:20), so that we may be ministers of reconciliation, "ambassadors for Christ" (see 2 Cor 5:17-20). To be ministers of reconciliation, we must first receive God's mercy and His forgiveness of our sins so that we may forgive as we are forgiven (see Mt 6:12). You cannot give what you don't have. Having received mercy, we are to give mercy from the heart (see Mt 18:35).

Reconciliation is so needed in our human condition! We are sinful, guilty, despondent, resentful, and divided, with deep feelings of unworthiness and shame.

Reconciliation lets mercy flow. We are reconciled to God and His Church by the Sacrament of Reconciliation, and to one another by mutual forgiveness.

In the Sacrament of Reconciliation, the priest acts in the Person of Christ and forgives the sins we bring. The priest prays in the name of God and the Church:

God, the Father of mercies, through the death and resurrection of his Son has reconciled the world to himself and sent the Holy Spirit among us for the forgiveness of sins; through the ministry of the Church may God give you pardon and peace, and I absolve you from your sins in the name of the Father, and of the Son, and of the Holy Spirit. Amen. (Rite of Penance)

What a miracle of mercy we have in this "Tribunal of Mercy"! This is not a court of law dispensing justice and condemnation with others accusing us; rather, it is a court of mercy, where we accuse ourselves and have the Holy Spirit as our defense lawyer and Jesus as our judge dispensing mercy. Our Lord told St. Faustina:

> **Tell souls where they are to look for solace; that is, in the Tribunal of Mercy. There the greatest miracles take place [and] are incessantly repeated.** (Diary, 1448)

As ministers and ambassadors of reconciliation, we can forgive others seventy times seven every day (see Mt 18:22). We can "broadcast" forgiveness to those in need by praying "Jesus, Mercy" at every occasion that calls for reconciliation, forgiveness, and mercy. This business of praying "Jesus, Mercy" becomes a full-time job!

We can pray with great trust for sinners who are in the greatest need of mercy. Our Lord told St. Faustina:

> **The greater the sinner, the greater the right he has to My mercy. . . . Pray for souls that they be not afraid to approach the tribunal of My mercy. Do not grow weary of praying for sinners.** (Diary, 723, 975)

"Holy Mary, Mother of God, pray for us sinners now. . . ." All of us are sinners, and we are in solidarity with the sin of the world, so we all need prayer for mercy.

Through the whole celebration of Mass, the Church prays for mercy, for the forgiveness of sin: in the opening penitential rite; in the solemn words of consecration; in the Lord's Prayer; in the plea "Lamb of God, you take away the sins of the world: have mercy on us"; and in the prayer before receiving Holy Communion: "Lord, I am not worthy to receive you, but only say the word and I shall be healed."

The sin and division in the Church and in the world are so rampant, and the times are so urgent, that we need God's mercy now! We need God's mercy to reconcile us to Himself, to His Church, and to one another.

Pope John Paul II, in his encyclical *Rich in Mercy* (15), strongly urges us to appeal to God's mercy now. Our Lord's words to St. Faustina also stress the urgency of appealing to this mercy:

> **Mankind will not have peace until it turns with trust to My mercy. . . . Speak to the world about My mercy; let all mankind recognize My unfathomable mercy. It is a sign for the end times; after it will come the day of justice. While there is still time, let them have recourse to the fount of My mercy; let them profit from the Blood and Water which gushed forth for them.** (Diary, 300, 848)

Now is the time to be reconciled. Now is the time to receive God's mercy and be merciful. Now is the time to be forgiven and to forgive.

chapter TEN

POWERLESSNESS

Being at a loss, powerless,
without purpose, without answers,
without faith, hope, or love.

vs.

Prayer

Asking continuously for God's mercy
and the power of the Holy Spirit
for ourselves and others.

Scriptural Response

" 'Ask . . . seek . . . knock. . . .' How much more will the heavenly Father give the Holy Spirit to those who ask him." (Lk 11:9, 13)

Response from St. Faustina

O my God, I am conscious of my mission in the Holy Church. It is my constant endeavor to plead for mercy for the world. (Diary, 482)

The good God entrusted her [the sister of St. Faustina] to my care, and for two weeks I was able to work with her. But how many sacrifices this soul cost me is known only to God. For no other soul did I bring so many sacrifices and sufferings and prayers before the throne of God as I did for her soul. I felt that I had forced God to grant her grace. When I reflect on all this, I see that it was truly a miracle. Now I can see how much power intercessory prayer has before God. (Diary, 202)

"Jesus, I beg You, by the inconceivable power of Your mercy, that all the souls who will die today escape the fire of hell, even if they have been the greatest sinners." . . . Jesus pressed me to His Heart and said, **You have come to know well the depths of My mercy. I will do what you ask, but unite yourself continually with My agonizing Heart and make reparation to My justice.** (Diary, 873)

Prayer as a Stepping Stone to Sanctity

How can prayer be an antidote to our needs? Probably the simplest answer to this question is the command of Jesus. He simply said, "Ask." He went on to explain:

> " 'Ask and you shall receive; seek and you shall find; knock and it shall be opened to you.' For whoever asks, receives; whoever seeks, finds; whoever knocks, is admitted. . . . How much more will the heavenly Father give the Holy Spirit to those who ask him." (Lk 11:9-10, 13)

And in our human condition, we have intense needs — so many people are powerless, without purpose, without answers, and, most importantly, without faith, hope, or love. The greatest need is for God's mercy, mercy that brings His forgiveness, His reconciliation, His salvation, His love. Only the Holy Spirit, the Spirit of Mercy, the giver of all "good things" (as described in Mt 7:11), can answer our real needs.

But our receiving God's mercy depends on our freely asking for it, because God so respects our freedom that He will not violate it. He waits for us to exercise our freedom by asking with trust for what we need. When we do this, we give God the freedom to act! By prayer, we give God permission to be merciful to us. And His mercy far exceeds our needs and our asking. His mercy is greater than our plans.

So when we pray, we allow God to fulfill His plan, in His way, and in His timing. And His plan is to have mercy on all (see Rom 11:32).

St. Faustina's life was dedicated to prayer, and she constantly asked for God's mercy for those in need. One of the prayers the Lord taught her to use was the Chaplet of Divine Mercy (see page 105), which He told her to say unceasingly (see Diary, 474). Awed by the effectiveness of this prayer, she wrote, "Never before had I prayed with such inner power" (Diary, 474).

The text of the Chaplet of Divine Mercy is a Eucharistic offering. It echoes the prayer of St. Michael at Fátima, and is like a "mini-Mass" that we can repeat throughout the day:

> Eternal Father, I offer You the Body and Blood, Soul and Divinity of Your dearly beloved Son, Our Lord Jesus Christ, in atonement for our sins and those of the whole world; for the sake of His sorrowful Passion, have mercy on us and on the whole world. (Diary, 476)

An even shorter form of asking for God's mercy is the simple exclamation, "Jesus, Mercy!" We cry out with our hearts, even as St. Faustina did, to Jesus, whose Heart was opened for us as the fountain of the Father's mercy. By this prayer, we not only honor Jesus as Divine Mercy itself, but we also ask Him to have mercy on us, on our present need, on the Church, and on the whole world. "Jesus, Mercy" can be a continual cry of our heart and our lips as we encounter the needs of the human condition. "Jesus, Mercy" is a mini-Chaplet, just as the Chaplet is a "mini-Mass."

Praying for God's mercy is also a stepping stone to sanctity. When we ask for mercy, we also ask for and receive the Holy Spirit, the Spirit of Mercy. It is the Holy Spirit who transforms us, who is poured into our hearts (see Rom 5:5) and makes us holy. The Holy Spirit transforms our earthen vessels, all our misery, into His temples! Holiness is not so much the vessel, as the content within the vessel; that is, the living presence of the Holy Spirit.

The more we ask for God's mercy, the more we are transformed into vessels of that mercy to a world in need. And there is no doubt that the world's greatest need is God's mercy — now!

This urgency is one of the major messages of Our Lord to St. Faustina, a message for the whole world:

> **Speak to the world about My mercy; let all mankind recognize My unfathomable mercy. It is a sign for the end times; after it will come the day of justice. While there is still time, let them have recourse to the fount of My mercy; let them profit from the Blood and Water which gushed forth for them.** (Diary, 848)

chapter ELEVEN

BURNOUT
Feeling persecuted, confused, tormented, distressed, tired, lonely, lost, trapped.

vs.

Merciful Heart of Jesus
Resting in the Heart of Jesus, seeking to unite our hearts to His.

Scriptural Response

"Come to me, all you who are weary and find life burdensome." (Mt 11:28)

"Put your hand into my side . . . [and] believe!" (Jn 20:27)

Response from St. Faustina

My daughter, know that My Heart is mercy itself. . . . No soul that has approached Me has ever gone away unconsoled. All misery gets buried in the depths of My mercy. (Words of Jesus, Diary, 1777)

When I see that the burden is beyond my strength, I do not consider or analyze it or probe into it, but I run like a child to the Heart of Jesus and say only one word to Him: "You can do all things." And then I keep silent. . . . (Diary, 1033; see also 1621, 1629)

The Merciful Heart of Jesus
as a Stepping Stone to Sanctity

If you are being attacked or persecuted, even by friends; if you are tormented, distressed, confused, fearful, tired out, burned out, weak, lonely, or just lost, then you need the refuge and rest that can only be found in the Merciful Heart of Jesus. Even if you can check off only one of the above, the antidote is still the same. The Merciful Heart of Jesus was opened up on the cross as a source of mercy, and as a stronghold for us in our attacked human condition.

The Lord taught St. Faustina to pattern her whole life on His Heart:

> **My daughter, I desire that your heart be formed after the model of My Merciful Heart. You must be completely imbued with My mercy.** (Diary, 167)

He made it clear to her that her life and mission had to be based on the union of her heart with His:

> **My spouse, our hearts are joined forever.** (Diary, 239)

Out of this union of hearts would flow His mercy:

> **My daughter, I desire that your heart be an abiding place of My mercy. I desire that this mercy flow**

out upon the whole world through your heart.
(Diary, 1777)

The most obvious characteristic of the life of St. Faustina was her intimacy with the Lord. This intimacy, this union of hearts, was the foundation of both her spiritual life and her mission as the secretary and Apostle of Divine Mercy. On every page of her diary, we see examples of this intimate union with God — how she loved Him, suffered with Him, talked to Him, and prayed to Him. Her whole life was preoccupied and possessed by God, who loved her with His tender mercy. She was often invited by the Lord to rest on His Heart, as did the beloved disciple (see Diary, 801, 929, 1348).

This intimate union with the Merciful Heart of Jesus is extended to us by the Lord Himself: "Come to me, all you who are weary and find life burdensome, and I will refresh you. Take my yoke upon your shoulders and learn from me, for I am gentle and humble of heart. Your souls will find rest, for my yoke is easy and my burden light" (Mt 11:28-30).

Like St. Faustina, we can surrender our hearts to the Merciful Heart of Jesus by our trust in Him; and thus, we, too, can live in an intimate union with Him. This is the Lord's desire and invitation. This is why His Heart was pierced for us on the cross as a fount of mercy. St. John, as an eyewitness to the piercing of the side of Jesus, tells us that it was done as a final sign so that we would look upon Him whom they have pierced and believe — believe with a committed faith (see Jn 19:33-37).

And so we are to cry out with Thomas's great cry of trust when he saw the pierced side and put his hand into the wound: "My Lord and My God!" (Jn 20:28).

We, too, like St. Faustina, are to rest on the Heart of Jesus, to live in the Lord, who is present to our hearts by the gift of the Holy Spirit (see Rom 5:5). What a merciful God we have, that He should be present to us in our human condition! When we are present to the Lord with our hearts, in the heart of our mother Mary, trusting and rejoicing, we can live in continual prayer, in continual intimacy with the Lord who loves us.

This intimacy of hearts with the Lord is a gift that is available for the asking! Each of us can implore, "Lord, change my heart. Make my heart like Yours. Lord, draw me, that I may be drawn. Fill me with the fire of Your divine love. Fill me with Your mercy, that I may radiate Your mercy to others. Come, Holy Spirit. Come, Lord Jesus!"

The Merciful Heart of Jesus is not only an antidote to our attacked human condition; it is the great stepping stone to sanctity, to our intimate union with God. In the Merciful Heart of Jesus, we learn and experience that God is mercy itself, that He is all in all, the first always and everywhere, the beginning and the end. He is the fire that enkindles our hearts with a living flame and transforms us (see Diary, 1050, 1140) so that "it is no longer I who live, but Christ who lives in me" (Gal 2:20, Revised Standard Version).

The intimate union of our heart with the Heart of Jesus means that we live in complete surrender to Him, seeking only Him. This is why He created us free, so that we may love Him and serve Him with our whole heart — freely.

This is why He permits us to fall in our human condition, so that we might turn to Him with our whole heart and receive His mercy. What He asks of all of us is to trust Him, so that He may be merciful to all (see Rom 11:32).

chapter TWELVE

INSECURITY
Feeling helpless, confused,
sad, sorry for self, unsure of self.

vs.

Mother of Mercy

Accepting the mother of Jesus
as our mother, too, allowing
her to comfort and form us.

Scriptural Response

"Behold, your mother." (Jn 19:27)

"Do whatever he tells you." (Jn 2:5)

Come children, hear me; I will teach you the
fear of the LORD. (Ps 34:12)

Response from St. Faustina

My daughter, at God's command I am to be, in a special and exclusive way, your Mother; but I desire that you, too, in a special way be my child. (Words of Mary, Diary, 1414)

My daughter, what I demand from you is prayer, prayer, and once again prayer, for the world and especially for your country. (Words of Mary, Diary, 325)

She [the Mother of God] has taught me how to love God interiorly and also how to carry out His holy will in all things. (Diary, 40)

O Mary, my Mother and my Lady, I offer you my soul, my body, my life and my death, and all that will follow it. I place everything in your hands. (Diary, 79)

The Mother of God told me to do what she had done, that, even when joyful, I should always keep my eyes fixed on the cross. (Diary, 561)

The Mother of Mercy as a Stepping Stone to Sanctity

Mary is the mother of Jesus and our mother. As His dying gesture of mercy on the cross, Jesus gave us His mother to be our own mother. He spoke to all of us when He said to the beloved disciple: "Behold, your mother" (Jn 19:27).

Our Blessed Mother told Faustina:

I am not only the Queen of Heaven, but also the Mother of Mercy and your Mother. (Diary, 330)

I am Mother to you all, thanks to the unfathomable mercy of God. (Diary, 449)

The Second Vatican Council teaches us that Mary, as the Mother of God, cares for us:

She is our mother in the order of grace. . . . Taken up to heaven she did not lay aside this salvific duty, but by her constant intercession continued to bring us the gifts of eternal salvation. By her maternal charity, she cares for the brethren of her Son. (Dogmatic Constitution on the Church, 61-62)

As our heavenly mother, Mary is the antidote to our insecurity, the Mother of Mercy, who, by her "maternal charity," helps us when we are helpless, confused, sorry for ourselves, sad, depressed, lonely, or lustful.

Yes, she can help us, because the Lord has chosen her to be an integral part of our redemption. The Father chose Mary to be the mother of His Son by the power of the Holy Spirit. Since God chose her, she is no longer an option on our part. Mary is ever mother. She is a powerful and necessary intercessor and mediator because of God's choice and plan. She carries out God's plan by the power of the Holy Spirit, her spouse. As mother, she continues to form us by the Spirit to be like Jesus. We go to Jesus the way He came to us — through Mary.

Anticipating the victory of the cross, Mary, conceived Immaculate in the womb of Anne, longs to share her special graces with her children — even the grace of her "Immaculateness." St. Faustina, after persistently asking it of Mary for many years, received the gift of purity, and was never again subject to temptations against it (see Diary, 40).

As the Mother of Mercy, Mary forms us, nurtures us, teaches us, guides us, and protects us. She can point to herself as the model of mercy and trust. And we can trust her because, as Pope John Paul II tells us, she is the "mediatrix of mercy" (*Mother of the Redeemer*, 41).

Like St. Faustina, we, too, can be "special" children of Mary (see Diary, 240, 1414). How? By asking for what we need and by entrusting our lives to Mary so that she may form us into the living image of Jesus. By entrusting our lives to Mary, we give her permission to act freely and bring us to the pierced Heart of Jesus on the cross, the source of all mercy. This is the meaning of consecration to Jesus through Mary. At the cross, by the radiance of His blood and water, we are transformed. We become living Eucharist and radiate His mercy. From Mary, we can learn to live the Magnificat, glorifying God, rejoicing in His mercy, and proclaiming it to every generation (see Lk 1:50).

One form of consecration to our Mother of Mercy is based on John 19:25-27. We can use it daily, asking Mary to be our mother and to form us as she formed Jesus by the Spirit:

An Act of Consecration to Mary

Mary, Mother of Jesus
and Mother of Mercy,
since Jesus from the Cross gave you to me,
I take you as my own.
And since Jesus gave me to you,
take me as your own.
Make me docile like Jesus on the Cross,
obedient to the Father,
trusting in humility and in love.
Mary, my Mother,
in imitation of the Father,
who gave His Son to you,
I, too, give my all to you;
to you I entrust all that I am,
all that I have, and all that I do.
Help me to surrender
ever more fully to the Spirit.
Lead me deeper into the Mystery
of the Cross, the Cenacle,
and the fullness of Church.
As you formed the Heart of Jesus by the Spirit,
form my heart to be the throne of Jesus
in His glorious coming.

AFTERWORD

What is the bottom line of the twelve antidotes and stepping stones? What does it all mean? What is the goal we should be trying to achieve?

The ultimate goal of all of our lives should be the union of hearts, the intimate union of our hearts with the Merciful Heart of Jesus by the transformation of His mercy. As the Holy Spirit is poured into our hearts, we are transformed into living Eucharist, and thus radiate His mercy to a world so much in need.

The very misery of our human condition is transformed by the Spirit of Mercy into something holy. It is like the Spirit of God that hovered over the chaos in creation (see Gn 1:2, Revised Standard Version) and brought forth light and life. The Holy Spirit hovers over our chaos to bring forth eternal light and life — the new creation. The Holy Spirit, the Spirit of Mercy, is the active agent of our sanctification. As Jesus offered Himself up through the Eternal Spirit (see Heb 9:14) and sanctified our suffering and misery into sacrifice bringing us salvation, so we, too, offer up our human condition through the Eternal Spirit to be transformed and sanctified, to become living Eucharist.

By the Holy Spirit, we are divinized, made members of the Body of Christ. It is a transformation that St. Faustina experienced and described in various ways. When she made the free oblation of herself and all her sufferings for souls, especially sinners, she experienced what she described as being "transconsecrated" (see Diary, 137). She prayed often to become a "living host" (see Diary, 642, 832, 1289, 1392, 1564, 1622, 1826), a small wafer, hidden and given in love, completely transformed into His mercy (see Diary, 514, 692).

How can we become apostles of Divine Mercy like St. Faustina? By living the twelve characteristic features of her spiritual life and mission, and by living the Sacred Scriptures as she did. She didn't write commentaries on the Word of God, but she was a living model of that Word.

In the Letter to the Hebrews, for example, we can see the scriptural foundation of the spirituality and mission of Divine Mercy recorded in the diary of St. Faustina. The author of the letter describes Jesus as the trustworthy and merciful High Priest, who identified Himself with His brethren in His passion, becoming victim and priest, offering Himself through the Eternal Spirit for the salvation of all. So by His mercy, He was "perfected," or transformed, and declared High Priest — in perfect relationship with God and mankind. He became the source of mercy for all who come to Him.

St. Faustina trusted in the merciful High Priest and totally identified with Him as victim, becoming a channel of His mercy to all in need. We, too, are invited to trust in Jesus, the merciful High Priest, and to unite with Him as victims of mercy for souls. Like Jesus and Mary, and like St. Faustina, we are called to humble obedience to the will of God.

As apostles of Divine Mercy, we, too, are to obtain and proclaim God's mercy as St. Faustina did (see Diary, 436), and so glorify the Divine Mercy as the very reason and purpose of our lives (see Diary, 1242).

Another way to live the message and mission of Divine Mercy is to fulfill the exhortations of St. Paul to the Thessalonians. St. Faustina did not comment on this text of the Word of God, but she obviously heard it and acted upon it:

Rejoice always. Pray without ceasing. In all things give thanks; for this is the will of God in Christ Jesus regarding you all. (1 Thes 5:16-18, Confraternity Edition)

- St. Faustina did, indeed, "*rejoice always.*" The main witnesses to this are the sworn testimonies of the sisters who lived with her (testimonies of witnesses for her beatification process). They were amazed how joyful she was in the midst of hard work and sickness.
- To "*pray without ceasing*" was the mission of her life (see Diary, 482). Mary taught her the importance of praying always: "*My daughter, what I demand of you is prayer, prayer, and once again prayer*" (Diary, 325). She prayed for sinners, priests, and souls in purgatory. Our Lord directed her: **"Say unceasingly the chaplet that I taught you"** (Diary, 687).
- "*In all things give thanks*" was expressed in the Eucharistic thanksgiving that was the center of St. Faustina's life. She especially gave thanks in suffering for souls (see Diary, 343), in the humiliations of her daily life (see Diary, 92, 593), and for everything (see Diary, 1367-69).

- *"The will of God"* was what St. Faustina sought with her whole will and life (see Diary, 374, 821, 652, 724, 821, 952). She completely united her will to His.
- *"In Christ Jesus"* — this was the foundation of her Apostolate of Divine Mercy, to be in union with the Merciful Heart of Jesus.
- *"Regarding you all"* — St. Faustina was told that what she wrote about the message of Divine Mercy was for all the souls throughout the world who would seek Him.

To live the word of rejoicing, praying, thanking always in Christ Jesus, is to trust the Merciful Savior and to live in union with Him, proclaiming and glorifying His mercy, like Mary, our mother; and like our sister, St. Faustina, the secretary and Apostle of Divine Mercy. It is to live the glorious Magnificat of Mary, to radiate His mercy as living Eucharist, to be an apostle of Divine Mercy.

Prayers

Litany of the Sacred Heart

Lord, have mercy.   **Lord, have mercy.**
Christ, have mercy.   **Christ, have mercy.**
Lord, have mercy.   **Lord, have mercy.**

God the Father in heaven,   **Have mercy on us.**
God the Son, Redeemer of the world, …
God the Holy Spirit, …
Holy Trinity, one God, …
Heart of Jesus, Son of the eternal Father, …
Heart of Jesus, formed by the Holy Spirit in the
     womb of the Virgin Mother, …
Heart of Jesus, one with the eternal Word, …
Heart of Jesus, infinite in majesty, …
Heart of Jesus, holy temple of God, …
Heart of Jesus, tabernacle of the Most High, …
Heart of Jesus, house of God and gate
     of heaven, …
Heart of Jesus, aflame with love for us, …
Heart of Jesus, source of justice and love, …
Heart of Jesus, full of goodness and love, …
Heart of Jesus, wellspring of all virtue, …
Heart of Jesus, worthy of all praise, …
Heart of Jesus, king and center of all hearts, …
Heart of Jesus, treasure house of wisdom and
     knowledge, …
Heart of Jesus, in whom there dwells the fullness of
     God, …
Heart of Jesus, in whom the Father is well
     pleased, …

Heart of Jesus, from whose fullness we have all
    received, ...   **Have mercy on us.**

Heart of Jesus, desire of the eternal hills, ...

Heart of Jesus, patient and full of mercy, ...

Heart of Jesus, generous to all who turn to you, ...

Heart of Jesus, fountain of life and holiness, ...

Heart of Jesus, atonement for our sins, ...

Heart of Jesus, overwhelmed with insults, ...

Heart of Jesus, broken for our sins, ...

Heart of Jesus, obedient even to death, ...

Heart of Jesus, pierced by a lance, ...

Heart of Jesus, source of all consolation, ...

Heart of Jesus, our life and resurrection, ...

Heart of Jesus, our peace and reconciliation, ...

Heart of Jesus, victim for our sins, ...

Heart of Jesus, salvation of all who trust in you, ...

Heart of Jesus, hope of all who die in you, ...

Heart of Jesus, delight of all the saints, ...

Lamb of God, you take away
    the sins of the world.   **Have mercy on us.**

Lamb of God, you take away
    the sins of the world.   **Have mercy on us.**

Lamb of God, you take away
    the sins of the world.   **Have mercy on us.**

V. Jesus, gentle and humble of heart,
R. Touch our hearts and make them like your own.

Let us pray,
Father, we rejoice in the gifts of love we have
    received from the heart of Jesus, your Son.

Open our hearts to share his life and continue
to bless us with his love. We ask this in the name
of Jesus the Lord.

R. Amen.

Chaplet of Divine Mercy

*The Lord revealed the Chaplet of Divine Mercy to
St. Faustina in September 1935. Here are the prayers
and the method for reciting it.*

The Chaplet of Divine Mercy is recited using
ordinary rosary beads of five decades.

1. Begin the Chaplet with one Our Father, one Hail
   Mary, and the Apostles' Creed.
2. Then, on the large bead before each decade, say:

   Eternal Father, I offer You the Body and Blood,
   Soul and Divinity of Your dearly beloved Son,
   Our Lord Jesus Christ, in atonement for our sins
   and those of the whole world.

3. Then, on the ten small beads of each decade, say:

   For the sake of His sorrowful Passion, have mercy
   on us and on the whole world.

4. Conclude with:

Holy God, Holy Mighty One, Holy Immortal
One, have mercy on us and on the whole world.
(three times)

(Adapted from *Mention Your Request Here*, by Michael
Dubruiel, © 2000 Our Sunday Visitor, Inc.)

A Consecration to the Sacred and Merciful Heart of Jesus

Lord Jesus, You invite me to come to You.
So I come to Your Sacred and Merciful Heart,
the fountain of all mercy,
with my sins, my misery, and my burdens.
Cleanse me, transform me,
and fill me with Your mercy.

Jesus, You invite me to take Your yoke.
So I take up my daily cross,
to walk in trust, in step with You.
I offer You my whole self as a living sacrifice.
Make me holy and acceptable to the Father
and make my heart like Yours.
As Your Heart was pierced for me,
pierce my heart to be a channel of mercy for others.

Jesus, You invite me to learn from You.
So teach me Your gentleness and humility.

As a child dependent on Your mercy,
I take refuge in Your Heart.
I want to do Your will and glorify Your mercy.

Jesus, You promised to refresh me.
So let me find peace
by resting on Your Heart like John.
I want to be present to You with my heart,
and radiate Your presence to others.

(By Rev. George W. Kosicki, C.S.B.,
© 1993, Marian Helpers)

Our Sunday Visitor . . .
Your Source for Discovering
the Riches of the Catholic Faith

Our Sunday Visitor has an extensive line of materials for young children, teens, and adults. Our books, Bibles, booklets, CD-ROMs, audios, and videos are available in bookstores worldwide.

To receive a FREE full-line catalog or for more information, call **Our Sunday Visitor** at **1-800-348-2440**. Or write, **Our Sunday Visitor /** 200 Noll Plaza / Huntington, IN 46750.

- -

Please send me: ___A catalog
Please send me materials on:
___Apologetics and catechetics   ___Reference works
___Prayer books   ___Heritage and the saints
___The family   ___The parish
Name_____
Address_____Apt._____
City_____State____Zip_____
Telephone (   ) _____

A23BBABP

- -

Please send a friend: ___A catalog
Please send a friend materials on:
____Apologetics and catechetics   ____Reference works
____Prayer books   ____Heritage and the saints
____The family   ____The parish
Name_____
Address_____Apt._____
City_____State____Zip_____
Telephone (   ) _____

A23BBABP

- -

Our Sunday Visitor
200 Noll Plaza
Huntington, IN 46750
Toll free: **1-800-348-2440**
E-mail: osvbooks@osv.com
Website: www.osv.com